CW00664971

E.Y. RIFLE AND CUP DISCHARGER

Top Photo—Showing position for discharging No. 36 Grenade
Lower Photo—Showing position for discharging No. 68

i

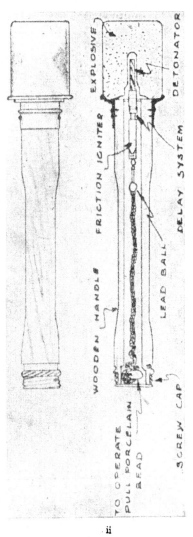

EXPLOSIVE

DETONATOR

FRICTION IGNITER

DELAY SYSTEM

WOODEN HANDLE

LEAD BALL

TO OPERATE
PULL PORCELAIN
BEAD

SCREW CAP

GERMAN STICK HAND GRENADE, No. 24

ii

GRENADES

FOR THE

HOME GUARD

AND THE

E.Y. RIFLE AND CUP DISCHARGER

By LIEUT. E. W. MANDERS
BATTALION WEAPON TRAINING OFFICER, H.G.

The Naval & Military Press Ltd

Published by

The Naval & Military Press Ltd
Unit 5 Riverside, Brambleside
Bellbrook Industrial Estate
Uckfield, East Sussex
TN22 1QQ England

Tel: +44 (0)1825 749494

www.naval-military-press.com
www.nmarchive.com

CONTENTS

ILLUSTRATIONS

4

CHAPTER I

BY WAY OF INTRODUCTION

GRENADES fall roughly into the following
groups:—
    (1) Anti-personnel,
    (2) Anti-tank,
    (3) Smoke and Incendiary.

The Home Guard are being increasingly issued with
grenades classified in all the three above-mentioned
groups. From this it will be understood that the Home
Guard have grenades to deal with enemy infantry,
A.F.V.s and light tanks, to put up a smoke screen and
also for demolition purposes.

The effectiveness of any infantry weapon is judged
by its lethal capacity and destructiveness, combined
with its mobility and handiness. The hand grenade,
judged by these standards, assumes tremendous
importance. It is easily carried by the average infantry-
man, in addition to his rifle or machine carbine, and
even one grenade is capable of inflicting a high per-
centage of casualties among a bunched enemy.

There is a tendency to allow drill to dictate the
weapon rather than the weapon to dictate the drill, and
as a number of new types of grenades are now being
issued, it is important that an open mind should be
kept on this subject, and full advantage be taken of the
respective merits of each particular grenade.

To classify all grenades under one heading is a
mistake, and each one should be studied individually.
This applies to officers in particular. They should
carefully study each grenade, taking into consideration
its purpose, so that they can readily direct the training
of their men to take full advantage of the various types
that are now issued.

• Should this knowledge not be properly absorbed, they might find that on active service they would have difficulty in directing the equipping of their men, taking into consideration the carrying capacity of the man in conjunction with the bulk and weight of each of the grenades. Handy methods of carrying the various grenades would have to be evolved, and considerable imagination and improvisation would have to be used in solving this problem.

Some grenades are more vulnerable to rifle fire and damage than others, and the writer suggests that grenades should always be carried so that they can be flung on one side quickly in an emergency. Bottle bombs, for instance, will require particular care in transportation. The writer will give some suggestions for the carrying of each particular grenade as it is dealt with, purely to direct a line of thought, and not to set up a criterion.

All ranks should be trained in the use of grenades, but, also, in addition, a bombing squad should be formed of picked men selected for their courage, determination, physical ability to keep up a sustained effort, and the ability to take care of themselves without direction. Combined with the above assets, they should also have a thorough knowledge of the working parts of each grenade and of all safety precautions.

A great deal of training is required to give a man confidence in the weapon and as much "live" throwing practice should be given as possible. Drill movements are invaluable at the commencement of training, but after a period, the men should be allowed to develop any particular style that suits them; also they should practise throwing from all positions.

Particular care should be taken in training men in the use of the No. 36 hand grenade, as once this grenade is grasped fully, in theory and practice, the men become bomb-minded and the other grenades come easily to them.

Bombing officers can do a great deal in training instructors and giving men practice; but, if, when the men return to their platoons, this practice is not kept up and full advantage taken during field exercises for the throwing of improvised or token grenades, then all the Bombing Officer's good work will have been wasted.

Whenever grenades are being handled, instructional, dummy or live, all safety precautions should be carried out, as a routine, in order to instil the habit in everyone concerned. Accidents do happen at times, and mostly these can be traced to the non-compliance with safety precautions. There is no more danger attached to the handling of grenades than there is in handling any other type of lethal weapon, providing that the handler has received, and absorbed, sufficient instruction, and, above all, uses his common sense.

Whenever the design of the grenade being handled permits it, always be sure to carry out the first SAFETY PRECAUTION, *i.e.*, remove the base plug and see whether the grenade is primed.

CHAPTER II

THE No. 36 H.E. GRENADE.

Group No. 1 – –	Anti-personnel.
Weight – – –	1 lb. 9 oz. approximately.
Dimensions – –	3¾ ins. × 2¼ in. approximately. 4 ins. × 2½ in. with the gas check fitted.
Explosive content –	Baratol is the main filling in those grenades issued to the Home Guard, but other explosive fillings are being used.
Lethal effect – –	By blast and fragmentation.
Type – – – –	Delayed action by time fuse: 4 seconds delay for hand-throwing; 7 seconds delay when fired from the Cup Discharger.
Packing – –	The hand grenades are packed 12 to an oblong wooden box marked "Hand Grenades 4 secs." and the type of explosive filling shown. With the grenades is a round tin box containing 12 igniter sets. Attached to the underside of the lid is found a base plug key. The rifle grenades are packed as above, but have "7 secs." marked on the box, and the box contains, in addition, 12 gas checks, and a tin containing 14 ballistite cartridges.

The No. 36 grenade was designed during the Great War 1914-1918 for trench warfare. So efficient did it prove that it still continues to be part of the Army equipment, and in the process it has undergone only slight modifications. Its mechanism is simple and safe, and troops can be rapidly trained to its use. It is small in size and can be fairly easily carried as compared with the enemy stick grenade.

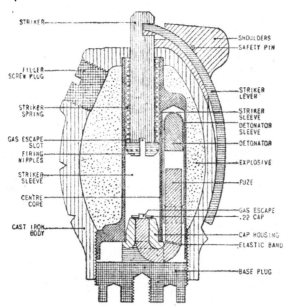

No. 36 H.E. HAND GRENADE

Designed, as it was, for trench warfare and having a large lethal area, it should be thrown from behind some sort of cover, which should be good enough to protect the thrower from any fragments that might fly in his direction. It is so effective, in both attack and defence, that all ranks should be trained to its use and not merely the men selected as expert bombers. With a gas check fitted, it can be fired from both the Discharger and the Northover Projector.

CHARACTERISTICS

Short Range (relatively).—It can be thrown by hand from 25 up to 35 yards. Fired from the Discharger, its range is from 80 up to 200 yards.

High trajectory with steep angle of descent.—Throwing or firing it in this manner gives it great searching power to clear trenches and breastworks. It also has less tendency to roll on landing.

Heavy Weight (relatively).—Owing to its weight (1 lb. 9 oz. only), a few can be carried by men in action; but supplies can be transported, in addition to other equipment, in battalion vehicles.

Large lethal area.—Up to 20 yards in all directions and on stony ground will wound up to 100 yards.

COMPONENTS

The Body.—The grenade consists of a cast-iron body, which is ovoid in shape and segmented to afford a grip and also to create a shrapnel effect upon the grenade bursting. Cast on, and to one side of, the body, are two shoulders, which have grooves cut in them to receive the trunnions of the striker lever, and these are also drilled to receive the safety pin. Through the top of the body a hole is drilled to receive the striker. Between the shoulders and running almost the full length of the grenade is a recess, which allows the striker lever to lie level with the surface of the body. Opposite to the shoulders a hole is tapped and threaded to receive the filler screw plug.

A hole is cast in the bottom through which the centre core is screwed into the inside of the body: this hole in turn is tapped and threaded to receive the base plug. The base plug is fitted with either two holes or two slots to receive the base plug key and is drilled and tapped centrally to receive the gas check (for use in the Cup Discharger).

The Core or centre-piece is constructed of a light metal alloy and is screwed into the inside of the body. At the head of, and inside, the body is a shouldered recess to receive the top end of the core.

10

The core consists of two sleeves, the larger of which (situated centrally) is drilled throughout its length and receives the striker and spring, whilst the smaller and outside one, which is sealed at its top end, receives the detonator. The base plug, when screwed into the body, retains the igniter set in position and seals the opening to the core.

The Striker is constructed so as to form a head and neck. The head is of a larger diameter than the neck, thus forming a shoulder, against which the striker spring bears. The head is formed with two firing nipples and between them a gas escape slot is cut. Towards the extreme end of the neck and in the normally exposed portion a slot is cut to receive the striker lever.

The Striker Spring is of the spiral compression type and surrounds the striker, and is compressed between the inside of the head of the grenade and the striker head.

The Striker Lever is shaped to lie in the recess in the body provided for it, and is formed with trunnions to fit into the slots in the shoulders. The trunnion end of the striker lever fits into a slot in the striker and is held in position by

The Safety Pin is a split pin fitted with a ring for withdrawal purposes.

The Igniter Set consists of a cap housing or chamber, a ·22 rim fire cap, a length of safety fuse and a No. 27 detonator.

The Cap Housing is shaped so that the upper portions in which the ·22 cap is fitted is of a slightly smaller diameter than the striker sleeve into which it fits. Around the middle is formed a shoulder of a larger diameter which rests against the underside of the striker sleeve. Through the centre runs a hole to receive the safety fuse. The bottom portion is grooved to form a protection for the safety fuse and the base plug screws tightly against it to hold the igniter set in position in the grenade.

The ·22 Cap is of the rim fire type and has a hole through its centre to form a gas escape. This hole is covered with a waterproof paper disc. This acts as a seal against damp.

The Safety Fuse has one end fitted tightly into the cap housing and cap, and the other into the detonator which is crimped tightly around it to form a damp-proof joint.

For Hand Throwing the fuse is **white** and around it is an elastic or paper band. Time of fuse, **4 seconds.**

For Firing from the Cup Discharger the fuse is coloured **yellow** and has no band fitted. Time of fuse, **7 seconds.**

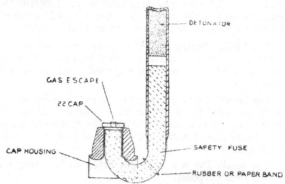

DETONATOR

GAS ESCAPE

22 CAP

CAP HOUSING

SAFETY FUSE

RUBBER OR PAPER BAND

IGNITER SET FOR No. 36 H.E. GRENADE

The Detonator (No. 27) is fitted and crimped to the fuse. Its explosive content may be either fulminate of mercury or lead azide. The more recent detonators contain the latter explosive.

RECOGNITION

A live grenade (i.e., one filled with explosive) is varnished either black or dark brown, and has a red band or a series of crosses painted around its upper portion at filler screw level, and around the middle is a coloured band denoting the explosive content.

The dummy, or practice, grenade is painted either white or grey, and as a general rule has holes pierced into the body.

MECHANISM

There is a striker spring held in compression between the shoulder of the striker and the head of the grenade. The striker is held by the striker lever, which, in turn, is held by the safety pin passing through the holes in the shoulders and over the striker lever.

Upon the safety pin being withdrawn the grenade remains perfectly safe *whilst the grip on it is maintained and the striker lever is held in position.* Upon the grenade being thrown, the striker lever flies off and the striker is free to be forced down by the compressed striker spring on to the ·22 cap in the igniter set. The cap is fired and the resultant flash ignites the safety fuse, which burns either 7 or 4 seconds, as the case may be, and then the detonator explodes and in turn explodes the main charge in the grenade. The resultant gases from the cap and fuse burning escape through the hole in the cap, the gas escape slot in the striker, into the striker sleeve and out through the hole in the top of the grenade into the open air.

EXAMINATION—STRIPPING AND CLEANING

Grenades and igniter sets should never be examined together. The igniter sets should be removed from the boxes and placed at a safe distance from the scene of operations and be examined separately.

First Safety Precaution.

(a) No grenade should be handled until the base plug has been removed in order to ascertain whether the grenade is primed or not, i.e., whether the igniter set is in position. Should it be primed the igniter set must be removed and placed in safety away from the scene of operations.

(b) Examine the body for cracks. If the grenade is cracked reject it, as damp may have damaged the explosive content.

(c) Examine the shoulders. If damaged or cracked the striker may be prematurely released.

(d) See that the striker lever lies snugly in the groove provided for it. If it stands out from the body the ring of the safety pin of another grenade may engage on it during transportation in a haversack or pouch, or on being placed in the cup discharger it may foul its edge.

(e) See that the striker lever properly engages in the slot in the striker.

(f) See that the safety pin is undamaged and free from rust.

(g) See that filler screw is properly luted and screwed fully home.

Stripping the Grenade.

The grenade may be examined as follows for faults or for cleaning purposes:

Hold the grenade with the lever in the palm of the hand at the base of the fingers and withdraw the safety pin. Place the open base end of the grenade against the waist band and release the striker lever, retaining same in the hand. This allows the striker and spring to fall. Tilt the grenade so that the base is uppermost before removing from the waist band, thus preventing the striker and spring from falling to the ground. Remove the striker and spring. The grenade is now stripped.

(a) Examine the centre core for cracks and see that the detonator sleeve is true and free from obstructions and of sufficient depth to take the detonator. A wooden gauge can be made for this important purpose. Thoroughly clean the striker and detonator sleeve and see that the core is free from rust.

NOTE:—Not so much importance is now attached to cracks in the partition between the two sleeves owing to the use of lead azide in the detonator. The writer has examined a number of grenades and has yet to find one with cracks in this portion. Under these circumstances it would seem wise to discard what few would be found to be faulty in this respect. Should the older type of detonator be used a flash from the

14

cap may pass through any such crack to the detonator, thus causing a premature.

(b) Examine the striker and see that it is not cracked at the striker lever groove. See that the head is intact with two firing nipples. See that the gas escape slot is cut into the head. Thoroughly clean and see that the striker is free from rust; leave lightly oiled, or greased with a light grease.

(c) Examine the striker spring for tension; clean and lightly oil as above.

(d) Thoroughly clean all luting away from the striker hole in the top of the grenade and from around the shoulders, and leave the body of the grenade free from dirt, luting and grease. If paraffin is used for cleaning purpose wipe the grenade dry. Use paraffin sparingly on body of grenade, and see that none enters the sleeves.

Re-assembling.

Replace the striker and spring and see that the slot in the striker faces between the shoulders. Next, by using a wooden dowel or dummy round, push the striker up, so compressing the spring until the slot in the striker neck can be engaged by the striker lever. Replace the safety pin. With the grenade held in the left hand, with the shoulders and lever to the front, insert the pin from right to left. Do not use a screwdriver or any sharp metal instrument to push up the striker, as damage to the striker sleeve may result.

(a) Before finally re-assembling, release the striker again to make sure that it works freely in its housing.

(b) Open out the ends of the safety pin.

(c) Replace base plug.

> NOTE:—It is always a good point to replace grenades in the boxes they originally came out of, so that, should any faults be found, same can be traced back.

The grenade is now ready for action, apart from priming.

Examination of the Igniter Set (7 and 4 seconds fuse).

The 4 seconds fuse is white for daylight recognition and the elastic band around it should on no account be removed, as this serves for recognition in the dark. The 7 seconds fuse can be recognised by its yellow colour in daylight, and by the absence of the rubber ring in the dark.

(a) See that the waterproof paper is intact and sealing the gas escape hole in the ·22 cap.

(b) See that the detonator is attached firmly to the fuse.

(c) See that the fuse is firmly fixed in the cap housing.

(d) When handling igniter sets always hold by the cap housing or fuse. *Never hold by the detonator.*

PRIMING

To prime the grenade, remove the base plug and insert the detonator into the small outside sleeve and the cap housing into the centre or larger sleeve, and replace the base plug and finally tighten it up with the key provided. Do not use too much force, or damage may be done to the core.

Precautions.

(a) Do not use force when inserting the detonator into its sleeve. If it will not fit in easily, discard the grenade.

(b) Should the igniter set be spread apart by the safety fuse, push it into position by holding it between finger and thumb, and see that the safety fuse is not pushed over a corner of the cap housing: otherwise, when the base plug is screwed home, the safety fuse may be damaged and the powder train broken.

The grenade is now primed and ready for throwing.

TACTICAL USES OF THE No. 36

(i) For clearing trenches, dug-outs, breastworks, machine gun posts.

(ii) For patrols. With each patrol sent out expert bombers should be included in the personnel.

(iii) **For street fighting.** For bombing the enemy out of houses, pill boxes, etc.

(iv) **For killing the crews of A.F.V.s** and for use against lorry-borne infantry.

(v) **For clearing woods,** for ambushes and all night fighting.

(vi) **For all close-quarter fighting,** offensive or defensive.

THROWING PRACTICE—STANDING

Strict discipline should be maintained during throwing practice, both for the benefit of the instructor and the men themselves.

A useful practice range can be set out as shewn in the following sketch:—

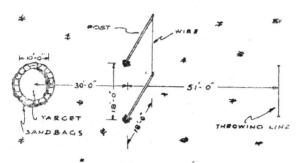

PRACTICE RANGE FOR HAND GRENADES.

Drill.

Though too much drill movement is to be deprecated, a certain amount at the commencement is beneficial. The following is a useful routine drill:—

Men on throwing line, at ease, with grenades at their feet on right (if left-handed, on left).

"Attention!—Pick up grenade—ready." (Then, individually)—"Prepare to throw—throw."

17

Analysis of Positions.

"Ready"—Hold the grenade in the right (or left) hand—as the case may be. With the lever under the base of the fingers, the thumb naturally assumes a position adjacent to the filler screw. Put the first or second finger of the other hand through the safety pin ring, and with the knuckles uppermost hold the hands close to the waist.

"Prepare to throw"—Withdraw the safety pin by pushing the right hand downward and to the rear, meanwhile keeping the left hand still. **Retain the safety pin on the finger until grenade has been thrown.** Glance towards the grenade to make sure that **all** the pin has been withdrawn.

"Throw"—Keeping the eyes on, or in the direction of, the target, with the shoulders in line, slightly bend the right knee, swing the right arm and body as far back as possible (raise the left foot if necessary), allow the left arm to come up naturally and point to the target, and, in one movement, swing quickly forward keeping the throwing arm as upright as possible and deliver the grenade.

> *NOTE:*—It is a good idea to follow through with the right arm towards the target to improve accuracy. Should the thrower throw off the target, a slight easing off of the position of the left foot will often correct this. Should the thrower not swing the throwing arm up vertically enough, this tendency can be checked in practice by bringing the arm up until the ear is touched, keeping the head in the normal throwing position.

The above is the normal practice for throwing from a trench or behind cover.

Throwing in the Open. When throwing in the open, the thrower should finish the throw in the prone position and as flat to the ground as possible. This can be done by continuing the forward movement of the throwing arm (after delivering the grenade) in a downward arc, meanwhile bending the body down-

18

wards, and also bending the knees (a collapsing movement) until the tips of the fingers and thumb of both hands are resting on the ground, then taking the weight on the outspread fingers push the legs and body backwards.

This is a modification of the present day "lying load" movement, and in the writer's opinion better than throwing one's self forward: as, in the latter case, selection of the ground to fall on cannot take place, and injury to hands may result from barbed wire and sharp stones or some other form of hidden obstruction. Continual practice should be given in this prone movement to get it done neatly and quickly.

An expert Army physical instructor on seeing this movement was enthusiastic and declared it to be an ideal movement for physical instruction, as it combined both movement and brain. One can also assume the prone position more rapidly by this method; and when under fire time counts.

Throwing the Grenade from the Prone Position.

This movement should also be practised, and the following is a simple drill movement to follow in the initial stages.

"*Ready*"—Adopt the prone position (face downwards) with head towards the target. The grip on the grenade is similar to that in the standing position. Place the index or second finger of the left hand through the safety pin ring with the arms slightly in front of the head so that all movements can be observed. Keep the whole of the body, head and legs close as possible to the ground.

"*Prepare to throw*"—Withdraw the pin.

"*Throw*"—Place the hands in a position to aid the upward movement of the body. Bring the right foot up towards the left knee, and, whilst keeping the left knee on the ground, push quickly up and swing the body back. Allow the left arm to rise, point towards the target with the shoulders in line and the right arm fully extended. Swing forward, at the same time bringing the right arm up (as for the standing throw), deliver the grenade and assume the prone position again as quickly as possible.

>*NOTE:*—One of the points to watch in this movement is that the feet are flat to the ground the same as in the prone position for firing the rifle. Constant practice is required to attain proficiency in the movement, and this is well worth while. A well-trained bomber can hurl a grenade from this position very nearly as far as from the standing position, and with as much accuracy.

Simplified Drill.—After proficiency has been obtained both for the standing and prone positions by using the drill described and the instructor is sure that the importance of observing that the pin has been properly withdrawn has been grasped, then the drill can be simplified by using only the following orders:—

"Ready"—This is as previously described with the "Prepare to throw" movement added to it, but the speed of the movement quickened up by cutting down the length of time required previously for seeing that the pin was properly withdrawn.

"Throw"—The same as previously described.

When the drill movements and throwing over the wire have been properly absorbed, training should be given in throwing from all positions, so that throwing from the standing, kneeling and prone positions can be practised. This can be done by throwing from cover of varying heights down to a shallow fold on the ground.

Practice should also be given throwing grenades in woods.

In street fighting grenades will be thrown through windows; therefore this should be practised as well as lobbing grenades out of windows. Once confidence in the weapon has been obtained, grenades can be lobbed by an underarm movement, or in any manner required by the emergency. Some men may be individualists and develop a style of their own; this should not be discouraged, particularly if the man has gained proficiency during drill movement and practice. During the latter part of training drill movements should be cut out altogether.

ADVICE TO THE BEGINNER

Above all, relax. Think of shadow-boxing and keep the weight slightly on the toes. Bend the knees slightly, take up a good balanced stance so that you get the feeling that a good shot will be the result. Do not hang about on the shot, swinging backwards and forwards: make the shot one continuous balanced movement. Follow the shot through and keep your eyes on the target. Straighten up the right leg at the point of delivery so that you can get every ounce of swing into the throw.

Don't worry if you cannot throw as far as others; practise and gain accuracy, which is essential. A 35-yard throw that misses the target is not so good as a 25-yard throw that hits it! Get to know your length of throw and approach your target until it is in range.

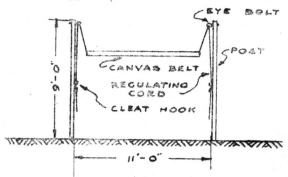

THROWING CORRECTOR SCALE ⅛″ TO 1′-0″.

Develop an easy type of throw without too much exertion so that if necessary you could bomb all day long. Always remember that in the hands of an expert grenades are deadly to the enemy, and that in the hands of a novice they can be deadly to your comrades and yourself.

Finally, all practice in the latter stages should be done in full battle order and *remember to tighten the chin strap of your helmet.* The writer, on more than one occasion, has seen accidents avoided only by a hair's-breadth through steel helmets being jerked forward over the eyes during live throwing. On one or two of these occasions spectacles have been knocked off and broken.

During a visit to a certain training school in Hertford-shire, the writer was particularly struck with a gadget that Captain Marques has erected to train novices to keep their right arms up during throwing practice. It consists of two posts between which is suspended a canvas belt, which is adjustable for height. The thrower stands under the belt with his right arm stretched fully up with clenched fist. The belt is adjusted to slightly under this height. The thrower then faces one of the supports, as facing a target, and goes through the motions of throwing (without grenade), and during the throw has to touch the belt with his knuckles, continuing the movement until the right hand touches the ground. (*See sketch, page* 21.)

METHOD OF CARRYING

A small quantity of special haversacks for carrying grenades have been issued. The ordinary Home Guard haversack is not strong enough for carrying grenades and should not be used unless it has been considerably strengthened. Riflemen could carry some grenades in that portion of the ammunition pouch not taken up by clips of cartridges. A canvas bucket makes an excellent receptacle for grenades, as the contents can be easily reached without groping.

One dozen of the No. 36 H.E. Grenades are about the most that a bomber should carry.

FIRING THE No. 36 H.E. GRENADE FROM THE NORTHOVER PROJECTOR

Ranging.—Add 50 yards to the actual range, e.g., for 100 yards actual range use the hole in the backsight for 150 yards range.

Loading.—Insert the grenade into the breach with the base plug first and the shoulders to the rear. When the grenade is inserted sufficiently for the striker lever to be held by the breach, remove the safety pin and push grenade fully home.

Fuse.—Prime the grenade with the 4-second igniter set.

Propellant Charge.—The ordinary propellant charge is used, but in this instance the soft rubber disc can be removed if so desired.

> *NOTE:*—For instruction in firing the No. 36 H.E. Grenade from the Discharger, see under "The Cup Discharger," page 26

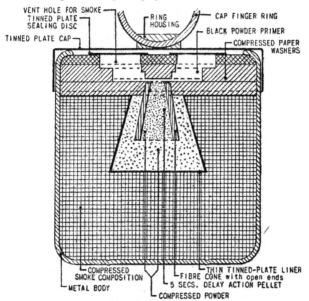

VENT HOLE FOR SMOKE
TINNED PLATE
SEALING DISC
TINNED PLATE CAP
RING HOUSING
CAP FINGER RING
BLACK POWDER PRIMER
COMPRESSED PAPER WASHERS
COMPRESSED SMOKE COMPOSITION
METAL BODY
FIBRE CONE with open ends
5 SECS. DELAY ACTION PELLET
THIN TINNED-PLATE LINER
COMPRESSED POWDER

No. 63 Smoke Grenade

CHAPTER III

THE No. 63 SMOKE GRENADE.
GROUP No. 3.

Weight, 1½ lb.; delayed action, 5 seconds; dimensions, 2½ inches × 2½ inches. Designed to be fired from the Cup Discharger.

Description.

This grenade consists of a strong, smooth, cylindrical metal casing, the top end of which is flattened off and inside a ring, shaped into this end, is stamped the word "TOP" and the edge of the grenade is rounded off. The bottom end is slightly recessed and has two holes pierced through it covered by two thin-tinned-plate discs about ⅜-in. diameter, soldered in position. This end is protected and covered by a tinned-plate cap. The flange of the cap is slotted and holed in four places so that the cap is sprung onto the body. In the centre of the top of the lid is attached a metal ring.

The grenade is filled with a smoke composition; at the open end is a primer in the middle of which is a 5-second delay action pellet.

Action.

The cap is removed by the ring designed for this purpose. This action exposes the bottom end to which the discs are soldered and the grenade is then loaded into the Cup Discharger with this end first.

Upon the rifle being fired the resultant explosion from the ballistite cartridge blows off the two tinned-plate sealing discs, allowing the the flash to ignite the delay pellet, which, after 5 seconds, ignites the primer. This in turn starts the burning of the smoke mixture. The mixture gives off a dense cloud of smoke for a period of approximately one minute.

Safety Precaution.

When firing from the No. 1 Mark I Cup Discharger, the two sealing discs are blown out of the gas port with a considerable force, and if this port is adjusted so that it is uppermost and towards the face of the firer, injury will be the likely result, unless the head is tilted downwards so that the face is protected by the brim of the steel helmet.

Recognition.

The No. 63 Smoke Grenade is painted an olive-green colour, and around the body towards the top end is a wide red band denoting a live grenade. Stencilled in black lettering around the body are the words, "Grenade 2·5" No. 63 Smoke E.1," and underneath this the word "Filled" in red letters, and the date of manufacture and lot number. In raised figures on the top of the lid is the number of the grenade.

Purpose of Design.

The function of this grenade is to lay a smoke-screen thus preventing observation and accurate fire by the enemy.

>   *NOTE:*—Owing to the relatively heavy weight of the grenade, only a few can·be carried; therefore, great care should be exercised in its use and not one single grenade should be wasted.

For method of firing and laying down a smoke-screen, see under "The Cup Discharger" in the following pages.

For Method of Carrying, see "No. 36 H.E. Grenade."

CHAPTER IV.

THE CUP DISCHARGER
(No. 1 MARK 1).

The Discharger No. 1 Mark 1 was designed to be used in conjunction with the No. 1 S.M.L.E. Rifle, and is generally known as the "Cup Discharger." With a special adapter fitted, it can also be used in conjunction with the ·300-inch (Pattern 1917 U.S.A.) Rifle. The Home Guard are generally equipped with this particular rifle; therefore, the following description applies to the discharger as fitted to it.

THE E.Y. RIFLE

The letters E.Y. are an abbreviation of the word "emergency," and the rifle is so called because, being a specially prepared rifle, it should be used to fire ball ammunition only in an emergency. It should be understood that the rifle, after being used to fire heavy grenades, becomes somewhat spoilt as a precision weapon. Ball ammunition can be fired from the rifle with the discharger fixed in position, but *only in an emergency* at very short ranges.

The discharger is inclined to work loose after firing a number of grenades. This effect should be watched for and the discharger readjusted. With the adapter fitted, it is doubly prone to work loose, and therefore a routine should be instructed whereby the discharger is readjusted after every four shots.

The Ballistite Cartridge.

The ballistite cartridge is a specially prepared ballless cartridge containing 30 grains of ballistite; the propellant charge is sealed into the case and then the end of the case is crimped up. This cartridge is the

ONLY ONE that should be used to fire live grenades from the discharger whether they be Nos. 36 and 63 or the anti-tank grenade.

Recognition.

The ·300 ballistite cartridge can be recognised, apart from the crimped end of the casing, by a blue splash on the cap. The cartridges are packed in a special cardboard container which is clearly marked describing the contents. .

Loading the Ballistite Cartridge.

The cartridges should on no account be pushed straight into the chamber of the rifle but loaded into the magazine, otherwise a broken extractor may be the result. The bolt requires somewhat heavier manipulation than when using ball ammunition, due to the fact that the cartridge lacks the assistance of the stream lined bullet as a guide, upon leaving the magazine to enter the chamber.

DESCRIPTION OF THE DISCHARGER

The discharger was designed, originally, to enable grenades to be propelled to a greater distance than when thrown by hand. In other words, when attached to a rifle it converted it into a light handy piece of artillery using as ammunition the No. 36 H.E. hand grenade. It is now used to fire the No. 36 H.E. Rifle grenade, the No. 63 Smoke grenade and also Signal grenades; and, in addition, it can be used for the No. 68 Anti-tank grenade. It is a magnificent addition to the Home Guard range of weapons and full advantage should be made of its several uses.

Make Up of the Discharger.

The discharger consists of a spun steel cylindrical smooth-bore barrel $5\frac{1}{4}$ inches in length by $2\frac{1}{2}$ inches in diameter. The barrel is sharply sloped in externally at the bottom to form a cam for the toggles to ride on. Near the lower end a slot is cut to form a gas port. The gas port is controlled by a sliding shutter, which can be fixed in any required position by a clamping nut.

Inside and at the bottom and tight against the barrel is fixed a portion of a ring forming a shoulder upon which the base of the grenade rests, thus keeping it clear of the gas port. Two circular studs are fitted inside at the bottom, which retain the gas shutter in

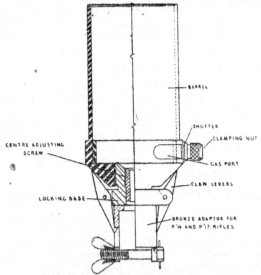

CUP DISCHARGER NO. 1, MARK I
Showing Adapter for P. 14 and P. 17 RIFLES

position when opened. The studs present only a small surface to the shutter, so that when the discharger becomes fouled upon firing it does not become jammed, as it would be if it ran in a deep groove. The barrel at its bottom end is concaved. At the bottom of the barrel a hole is drilled and tapped to receive the locking base.

The Locking Base.

The locking base has an upward projection which is threaded externally to screw into the barrel and down the centre is a hole which is threaded to receive the fine adjustment screw which has a hole running centrally throughout its length, approximately the same bore as the rifle barrel. The fine adjustment screw is slotted at its top end to receive the bayonet point, which is used as a screw turn. At one side of the base is a circular recess which fits against the dummy bayonet boss on the adapter, and on two opposite sides are fitted levers or toggles which rest against the cam of the barrel at their top end and are shaped like claws at the bottom and to engage in the slotted sides of the adapter.

The Adapter consists of a casting which is shaped in such a manner that when fixed to the top of the Pattern '17 rifle converts it to approximately the same shape as the top portion of the S.M.L.E. (*See sketch on page 28.*)

The barrel of the rifle fits into a hole through the top of the adapter, leaving the barrel slightly proud of the top surface and a dummy bayonet boss projects above the top of the adapter, and opposite to this is another projection, but flat in shape. Two sides of the adapter are slotted to emulate the slots in the cap of the S.M.L.E. and two holes are drilled through the sides of the adapter, which receive a bolt fitted with a wing nut. This bolt passes under the foresight protection blades of the Pattern '17 rifle after the adapter has been fitted on the end of the rifle, thus retaining the adapter in position.

To Fix the Discharger.

(a) Remove the bolt from the adapter. Place the adapter over the top of the rifle and re-insert the bolt and tighten up the wing nut. The adapter is now fixed.

(b) With the bayonet, slacken off the fine adjustment screw of the discharger until it is about $\frac{1}{8}$-inch shy of the underneath face of the locking base.

(c) Place the discharger on the adapter, taking care to get the circular recess in the locking base against and partly around the dummy boss of the adapter.

(d) Engage the claw ends of the levers into the slots of the adapter and hold them there with the left hand.

(e) With the right hand at the top of the barrel screw home the barrel until it is tight (do not use undue force).

(f) Insert the bayonet into the slots in the fine adjustment screw and screw fully home.

The discharger is now fixed.

To Unfix the Discharger.

(a) Slacken off the fine adjustment screw with the bayonet, so that it is somewhat in the position for refixing, i.e., $\frac{1}{2}$-inch shy of the base.

(b) Hold the levers with the left hand as in fixing. Unscrew the discharger with the right hand a sufficient number of times for the claws on the levers to disengage from the slots in the adapter, when the top ends of the levers are pressed inwards. Lift the discharger from the adapter.

(c) Remove the butterfly nut from the bolt of the adapter and withdraw the bolt. Next remove the adapter from the top of the rifle and replace the bolt into the holes in the adapter and screw on the wing nut.

RANGE SETTING

When firing the No. 36 H.E. Rifle grenade or the No. 63 Smoke grenade the rifle must be held at an angle of 45 degrees. The range is obtained by regulating the gas shutter in the gas port. With the gas port fully closed the maximum range is obtained; inversely, when the gas port is fully open the minimum range is obtained.

The reason for this is that when the port is closed no gas, resultant from the explosion of the cartridge, is allowed to escape prematurely, thus the whole force of the explosion is used to propel the grenade. When the gas port is opened a proportion of the gases escape and have no influence towards propelling the grenade. Measuring from the inside of the shutter each quarter opening of the gas port gives a difference in range of 30 yards.

GAS PORT	RANGE
Fully open	80 yards
Threequarters open	110 yards
Half open	140 yards
Quarter open ...	170 yards
Fully closed ...	200 yards

The clamping nut should be tightened up after each adjustment.

It should always be remembered that the wind has a big effect on range and aiming. For a cross wind you must lay off, and when firing into the wind a smaller gas port opening must be used than normally.

CARE AND MAINTENANCE

(a) Wipe the discharger over frequently with an oily rag to keep free from rust.

(b) After firing, strip the cup discharger right down, clean off all fouling from the barrel and from around the shutter. Treat all screws and threads in the same way until thoroughly clean. Well oil all threads and re-assemble. Finally, wipe over outside and inside of barrel with an oily rag. If this is not done the fine adjustment screw will seize up, making adjustment impossible.

(c) Should the discharger be contaminated by gas, it will be dealt with at the same time as the rifle and in the same way, taking particular care to cleanse all threads thoroughly. Finally, oil as before.

THE DISCHARGER No. 2, MARK 1

The No. 2 Mark 1 discharger is a modification of the No. 1 Mark 1. It was designed to overcome the inherent faults in the latter mark and to enable the adapter, as used with the ·300-inch (Pattern 1917 U.S.A.) rifle, to be dispensed with. It can be used in conjunction with the No. 1 (S.M.L.E.) the No. 3 (Pattern 1914) and the ·300-inch (Pattern 1917 U.S.A.) rifle.

It consists essentially of a barrel and a base.

The Barrel.—At the lower end and outside the barrel is a movable ring controlled by a locking bolt. The ring has four holes drilled through it to correspond with four holes in the barrel. By sliding the ring round to cover or uncover these holes various ranges can be obtained. Maximum range is obtained by covering all the holes and locking the ring into position.

At the bottom of the barrel there is an extension piece which is drilled throughout its length and having approximately the same bore as the rifle, and the lower end of it rests on the barrel of the rifle. At one side it is cut away so as to miss the bayonet boss when fixing on to the No. 1 (S.M.L.E.) rifle. The barrel screws into the base.

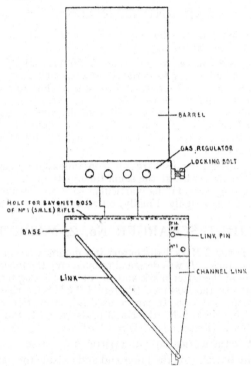

CUP DISCHARGER No. 2, MARK I

The Base.—The base is more or less U-shaped and the upper portion is drilled in two places. The smaller hole towards one end is for the bayonet boss of the No. 1 (S.M.L.E.) rifle to fit into, and the larger and

32

central hole is threaded to take the screwed extension of the discharger barrel. In the sides at the end which is holed for the bayonet boss are drilled two sets of holes, one above the other. Against the uppermost hole is stamped P.14 and at the lower No. 1.

A set of holes is drilled through the sides of the base at the opposite end to receive the two arms of the link.

The Channel Link, which is roughly U-shaped, is attached to the sides of the base by the channel link pin, which can be inserted into either set of holes provided for it. When the discharger is fixed to the No. 3 rifle (Pattern 1914) the upper set of holes is used, and when it is fixed to the No. 1 (S.M.L.E.) rifle the lower set of holes is used. The lower ends of the channel link are shaped to receive the bar of the link.

The Link is circular in section and is roughly U-shaped. The ends of the "U" are sharply bent over at right angles inwards to fit into the set of holes in the base provided for this purpose; the other end forms a bar which fits over the ends of the channel link.

RANGE SETTING

When firing the No. 36 H.E. grenade or the No. 63 smoke grenade the rifle is held at an angle of 45 degrees and the various ranges are obtained by rotating the gas regulator ring thus:—

ADJUSTMENT		RANGE
Four holes uncovered	...	80 yards
Three holes uncovered	...	110 yards
Two holes uncovered	...	140 yards
One hole uncovered	...	170 yards
All holes covered ...	...	200 yards

To manipulate the gas regulator ring, loosen the locking bolt and rotate the ring to the required setting, then retighten the locking bolt.

To Fix the Discharger.

The discharger barrel is unscrewed from the base about six turns. Adjust the channel link and the link so that the bar at the bottom of the link rests outside the channel link and rests in the housings provided for it, and over the bayonet standard. Then screw down the barrel of the discharger with the fingers, taking great care not to use excessive force, otherwise the barrel of the rifle may be damaged.

To Unfix the Discharger.

Unscrew the discharger about six or more turns and swing the channel link and the link clear of the bayonet standard, and remove the discharger complete.

FIRING POSITIONS AND LOADING FOR Nos. 1 AND 2 DISCHARGERS

For firing the No. 36 grenade prime the grenade with the 7-second igniter set, which has a yellow coloured fuse, which is not fitted with a rubber band. (See previous description under "The No. 36 H.E. Grenade.") After inserting the igniter set, screw home the base plug. Then screw the gas check, which is a circular disc 2½ inches in diameter, into the base plug, making sure that it is screwed home tight. The grenade is now ready for inserting into the discharger. The discharger has already been fixed to the E.Y. rifle.

Kneeling Position.

(a) Take up a kneeling position behind cover facing the target, with the left knee up and the right knee to the ground.

(b) Should the rifle be loaded with ball ammunition, unload and reload with ballistic ammunition and apply safety catch.

(c) Adjust the gas shutter No. 1 Mark 1 to the required range. In the case of the No. 2 Mark 1 discharger, rotate the gas regulator ring to the required position for the range required.

(d) Load the grenade into the discharger, gas check first, until the striker lever is held by the cup and withdraw the safety pin, retaining it upon the finger.

(e) Hold the rifle at an angle of 45 degrees with the rifle inverted, i.e., with magazine uppermost and the heel of the butt on the ground, keeping the left hand above and clear of the top band, then lightly clench the right hand with the index finger extended and through the trigger guard and resting on the trigger. On no account grip the small of the butt.

(f) Ease off safety catch and depress trigger.

Unload.

Should the grenade not be fired, the first thing to be done is to render it safe, i.e., to replace the safety pin. To do this, withdraw the grenade slightly from the discharger until the safety pin can be replaced. Then withdraw the grenade from the discharger and open out the ends of the safety pin on the edge of the discharger.

GENERAL NOTES AND HINTS FOR PRACTICE FIRING

(a) To check the angle of the rifle, hold the bayonet vertically at the upper band with the point on the ground. This should give an angle of approximately 45 degrees.

(b) A good method to adopt in practice to obtain an angle of 45 degrees with the E.Y. rifle is to kneel with the left knee up and the right knee to the ground, taking care that the left leg, up to the knee, is vertical to the ground, and the right leg from the knee to the hip is also truly vertical, thus roughly forming a square with the right thigh, the left leg and thigh and the ground. The left forearm should rest on the upper portion of the left thigh and horizontally to the ground.

Remember to hold the rifle with the left hand clear of metal portions. The heel of the butt should rest on the ground close to, and at the side of, the right knee and in line with it. The rifle thus assumes a position cutting diagonally from the right to the left knee.

(c) To reload ballistite, it is a good idea to bring the rifle up and lay it across the left thigh with the bolt uppermost. The bolt can then be easily manipulated and loading is made easier.

(d) Faulty alignment usually causes the grenade to go to the left of the target.

(e) Flinching when firing usually causes the grenade to go to the right.

(f) Full range discipline should be followed when firing both live and dummy grenades, and the command should be given to load, fire and reload. *Remember the safety catch.*

· (g) Remember that on firing the Nos. 36 and 63 that the rifle is inverted, i.e., bolt downwards and towards the ground.

(h) Allow for wind, which has a considerable effect on the flight of the grenade.

(i) *Areas* should be selected as targets, and not points.

(j) Though only one position has been given for firing, the writer has been to official demonstrations where, in addition, grenades have been fired from the shoulder and the hip. To fire from the shoulder the body should be carried with the shoulders well forward.

FINAL NOTE: DRILL MOVEMENT ·

The method for firing grenades has been considerably simplified and drill reduced to a minimum. The kneeling position has proved the best, and it will be noticed that the sitting position has been cut out. In the early stages of training, should a drill movement be preferred the orders should be given in the following order:—

The position should be behind cover with bayonet fixed.

Rifle Bomber.—Withdraw rifle from parapet, unfix bayonet, unload ball, reload ballistite, apply safety catch. Fix discharger.

Range.—Give target and range. Set range on discharger.

Load.—Load grenade as previously described. Keep the rifle canted upwards.

Unload.—Unload as previously described.

Rifleman.—Unfix discharger; fix bayonet, unload ballistite—reload ball—apply safety catch. Return to original position.

The writer considers that the above drill is unnecessary for the Home Guard, as in action the rifle bomber would have the discharger fixed to his rifle, and, even if not, he would not be used as a rifleman.

The only orders required are:—

Load—Target—Fire or Unload

Tactical Uses.

(a) To search behind cover.

(b) For use against machine gun posts.

(c) For street fighting, firing grenades through windows, etc.

(d) For putting up a smoke screen.

(e) To support the Northover Projector and other sub-artillery.

(f) For use against enemy tanks and vehicles.

(g) A great deal of live and dummy practice is required to give the rifle bomber confidence in the weapon. He should be used as much as possible on tactical exercises.

THE FIRING · POSITIONS AND PREPARATION FOR FIRING No. 68 ANTI-TANK GRENADES

Sight.

For firing No. 68 Anti-tank Grenades a special sight has been designed which fits just in front of the outer band in the case of the Pattern 1917 and No. 3 rifles, and just behind the outer band on the No. 1 rifle. (*See Sketch, page* 38.)

The top rim of the grenade should show level with the step used.

Ammunition.—30-grain ballistite cartridge.

Firing Position.

The best position for firing is the prone, i.e., with the left hand holding the rifle, and stomach to the ground. The rifle is held in the normal way with the bolt uppermost and at a low angle. Care should be taken to keep the hands clear of all metal parts of the rifle. On firing there is considerable recoil and the butt of the rifle should be held tightly against a filled sandbag or a hole should be made in the ground to receive it.

The safety catch having been pushed forward, lightly clench the right hand with the index finger

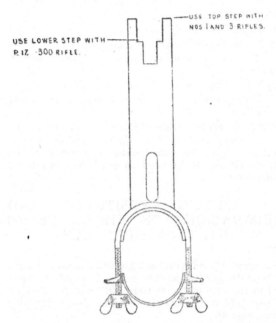

TOP OF GRENADE SHOULD BE LEVEL WITH TOP OF STEP USED.

No. 68 GRENADE RIFLE SIGHT, MARK II.

extended, take aim quickly and fire by pressing the trigger with the index finger. On no account hold the small of the butt in the normal way. The head must be held well back to take advantage of the sights and to keep the chin clear of the rifle. (*See frontispiece, page i.*)

Apart from this position, various types of cover can be used. The discharger can be fired from trenches, ditches and banks. In the case of a slit trench the butt is placed against the side of the trench and held tightly against it. In taking up these various positions the imagination must be used. Should the discharger be used in street fighting, it can be fired from inside a building, providing that something sufficiently heavy is used to support the butt; care should be taken to see that some kind of a pad is improvised to take the butt and save it from harm on recoil.

It should be explained in practice that the grenade must strike the tank squarely, otherwise it will glance off and damage the tail rendering the grenade useless.

TO LAY A SMOKE SCREEN WITH THE DISCHARGER, USING THE No. 63 SMOKE GRENADE

Positioning, etc., in all cases, are as used for firing the No. 36 grenade previously described.

Loading.

Remove the cap by the ring provided and load with the end, thus exposed, first. Ballistite cartridges are used to fire the grenade.

Purpose.

(i) The object of using a smoke screen is to keep down accurate return fire from the enemy and to render observation by him as difficult as possible. This should be done in such a way as not to impede or hamper the action of one's own troops.

(ii) Owing to the weight of the grenade, $1\frac{1}{4}$ lb., only a few can be carried; therefore, they should be applied only after full consideration has been given to the strength and direction of the wind, and the benefits that might be derived from their application.

Wind Direction.

(a) The best conditions are those appertaining when a cross wind prevails. Fire three or four grenades so that the smoke blows across the enemy position.

(b) Should the wind be blowing towards the enemy position, more grenades will be required. To allow the smoke to extend fanwise, the grenades should be fired to land about 100 yards in front of the position to be blinded. In this case, two or three grenades will be ample.

(c) Should the wind be blowing towards your own position it is not advisable to use smoke.

Laying a Smoke Screen.

(i) To start a smoke screen fire two grenades as quickly as possible. The grenades should be planted about 50 yards upwind away from the target area to allow the densest part of the screen to accumulate in front of the enemy position.

(ii) Feed the screen by firing grenades, about every half-minute, when the wind is normal. For a high wind increase the rate of fire to suit the conditions.

NOTE:—The No. 63 smoke grenade burns for about one minute.

CHAPTER V

THE No. 73 ANTI-TANK GRENADE (HAND) GROUP 2.

Type – – – –	Blast, percussion. H.E. (explodes on impact).
Weight – – – –	4 lb.
Dimensions – –	3¼ inches diameter by 11¼ inches in length.
Explosive Content –	3¼ lb. gelignite (nitro-glycerine gelatine dynamite).
Packing – – –	The grenades are packed ten to a tin box, including ten detonators in a cylindrical container.

Purpose of Design.

The use of this grenade is to attack and damage armoured fighting vehicles. The grenade is most effective when applied to the tracks, bogie wheels or suspension of a tank. Owing to its weight (4 lb.) and shape it cannot be thrown great distances. From 10 to 15 yards is the average throw. With plenty of practice an expert would, of course, improve on these figures. Owing to its short range and the powerful nature of the explosive content, it should be thrown from behind cover. Normally, it should be used in conjunction with road blocks and ambushes. At the end of this chapter the writer will go more fully into some of the ways in which this grenade can be applied.

Recognition.

The live grenade is painted a light buff colour and around the body towards the top is a red band. Stencilled in black on the body is a description of the grenade. The lid is sealed to the canister by white adhesive tape. The bakelite safety cap is also held to the lid by a strip of white adhesive tape.

The drill or dummy grenade is painted white.

Packing. Ten grenades packed in a tin box. Enclosed with the grenades is a cylinder containing 10 detonators.

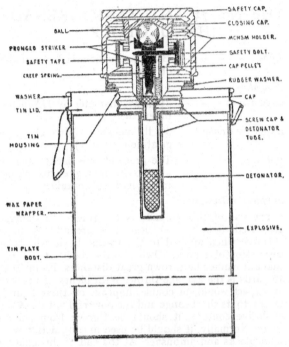

No. 73 Anti-Tank Grenade

DESCRIPTION

The Body consists of a cylindrical tinned-plate casing which contains the explosive. The top is threaded to receive the lid. Inside at the bottom is a corrugated paper washer.

42

The Explosive Content consists of 3¼ lb. of nitro-glycerine gelatine dynamite wrapped around with a waxed waterproof paper. At the top, bored into the explosive, is a hole to receive the detonator tube. In some cases, a further paper washer is found to fit under the lid.

The Lid, of tinned-plate, screws on to the top of the body. Soldered to the underside in the centre is a tinned-plate housing which is threaded internally to receive the bakelite mechanism holder and screwed externally to receive the detonator holder or tube. Sealing the lid to the body is a length of white adhesive tape which serves to exclude moisture and helps to retain the lid in position.

The Detonator Tube of tinned-plate is considerably larger in diameter at the top and this portion is shaped to screw on to the housing under the lid. The actual tube, into which the detonator is inserted, is of a considerably smaller diameter and is attached to the underside of the larger portion.

The Bakelite Mechanism Holder contains the "Always Fuse" and screws into the housing provided for it in the lid. Between the mechanism holder and the lid is a rubber sealing washer which serves to exclude moisture and forms the sealing for the holder and safety cap.

The "Always Fuse" consists of the following component parts:—

Bakelite mechanism holder.
Bakelite safety cap.
Bakelite closing screw cap.
Safety bolt and tape and bob-weight attached.
Pronged needle-pointed striker and cup.
Lead alloy ball.
Creep spring.
Cap pellet.
Percussion cap.

The Bakelite Mechanism Holder consists of a bakelite body which is recessed around its middle to form a "gallery" which in turn has two slotted holes drilled through it to receive the safety bolt.

The Safety Bolt, which is inserted through only one of these holes and engages through a hole drilled for it in the striker. Attached to the safety bolt is a length of tape about 8 inches in length which has attached to it in turn a bob-weight which is curved slightly to conform with the contour of the gallery. The safety tape and bob-weight are held in position by the bakelite safety cap.

The Bakelite Safety Cap, which is screwed to the holder by a quick release screw thread and is retained in position by a strip of adhesive tape. This adhesive securing tape denotes that the fuse is fitted with a live percussion cap.

The Screwed Closing Cap, which is concaved on its underneath portion, retains the internal mechanism in position and rests directly over and around the lead alloy ball.

The Lead Alloy Ball, which is equivalent in weight to the cap pellet, rests in a cup formed at the upper portion of the pronged striker.

The Pronged Striker has a cup formed at its upper end which is similarly shaped to the under portion of the screwed closing cap. Below this is a portion having a smaller diameter than the cap and through which is drilled a hole to receive the safety bolt.

Below this, in turn, is a further extension of a smaller diameter still, thus forming a shoulder. The extreme end of the striker is forked and each prong thus formed is needle-pointed. Around the striker is fitted the creep spring.

The Creep Spring is a light spiral spring which has sufficient tension to keep the lead alloy ball located against the underside of the screwed closing cap when the safety bolt has been withdrawn. It is located, in tension, between the shoulder of the striker and a shoulder in the sleeve of the cap pellet.

The Cap Pellet is made of brass and consists of a cylindrical rod bored throughout its length. Its lower end is chamfered externally to fit the lower internal portion of the mechanism holder. The sleeve has three internal dimensions. The upper is greater than the middle,. thus forming a shoulder against which rests the creep spring, and the lower of a greater diameter than the middle of the sleeve forms a housing for the percussion cap.

The Percussion Cap is of the ordinary rim fire type.

ACTION OF THE "ALWAYS FUSE"

The safety cap is removed and the grenade is thrown. During the flight of the grenade the bob-weight causes the tape attached to the safety bolt to stream out behind and unwind from the gallery of the mechanism holder until it finally withdraws the safety bolt. The safety bolt assembly then falls to the ground.

During the remainder of the flight, the striker is kept from contact with the percussion cap by the tension of the creep spring pressing the striker and lead alloy ball upwards against the closing cap, and the cap pellet downwards against the bottom of the mechanism holder. It is aided somewhat by the small depressions in the concaved portion of the cup of the striker and the closing cap. (Remember that the lead alloy ball and the cap pellet are equivalent in weight.)

(a) Should the grenade fall on its base, the resultant jar causes the lead alloy ball to overcome the tension of the creep spring and force the needle points of the pronged striker down on to the percussion cap (the striker has a very small amount of travel before hitting the cap). The resultant flash from the cap going off explodes the detonator which, in turn, causes the H.E. filling of the grenade to explode.

(b) Should a grenade fall on its top end, the resultant jar causes the cap pellet to overcome the tension of the creep spring and carry the cap on to the needle points of the pronged striker, thus firing the percussion cap.

(c) Should the grenade fall on its sides, the resultant jar causes the lead alloy ball to roll slightly down the inclined planes of the concaved portions of the cup of the striker and the closing cap, thus forcing them apart and at the same time forcing the needle points of the pronged striker on to the percussion cap.

Safety Precaution.

(a) Remove the lid without disturbing the safety cap and then unscrew the detonator·tube to ensure that the grenade is not primed.

(b) See that the detonator tube is free from obstructions.

Priming the Grenade (before throwing).

To prime the grenade, remove the adhesive tape, which is sealing the lid to the body, taking care to preserve it. Unscrew the lid from the body (without disturbing the safety cap of the "Always Fuse".) Replace the adhesive tape around the screwed portion at the top of the body, keeping the two ends of the tape down scarf fashion. Unscrew the detonator tube from its housing underneath the lid and insert the detonator into the tube CLOSED END FIRST. Screw the detonator tube back on to its housing. Then carefully insert the tube centrally into the hole in the explosive made to receive it and screw the lid on to the body. The grenade is now primed.

> *NOTE:*—Teach the replacing of the adhesive tape over the screwed top of the body in the manner before mentioned as a *routine* and *stress* it, as by this means one can tell at a glance that the grenade is primed. On disarming, i.e., removing the detonator from the grenade, always make sure to replace the tape so as to seal the lid to the body.

METHOD OF THROWING THE GRENADE

(i) Strip off the adhesive tape, which fastens the safety cap to the lid, and remove the bakelite safety cap *MAKING SURE THAT THE SAFETY TAPE AND BOB-WEIGHT ARE IN POSITION.*

(ii) Lay the grenade along the forearm with the mechanism holder towards the hand and retain the safety tape in position by a finger to prevent it unwinding.

(iii) Throw the grenade with an overarm action, similar to the action of a rugby player passing or throwing in.

(iv) Get down behind cover at once, i.e., without observing the impact of the grenade on to the target.

> *NOTE:* Throw the grenade well up, if used on soft ground, to ensure that there is enough force, on impact, to cause the mechanism to function. Though the grenade is often thrown in the open by instructors, it is inadvisable for the average thrower to do so and stress should be lain on the fact that cover should be taken.

Storage.

The grenades should be kept in a dry even temperature and on no account must the H.E. filling be exposed to moisture. The explosive content is highly inflammable. On a post care should be taken to keep the grenade under cover, as it is highly sensitive to rifle or machine gun fire, and, if possible, the grenades should be placed six feet apart.

Method of Carrying.

A stout canvas grenade haversack is, of course, the best way of carrying, but, if not available, a substitute can be made out of two sandbags strung together lengthwise and forming pockets for the grenades. A stout cord or a length of webbing can be attached for carrying. Three is the maximum that should be carried in this manner, but preferably only two.

Practice-throwing.

Hardwood dummies can be made to the same dimensions as the grenade, including, of course, the mechanism holder. Discarded safety bolts and tapes complete can be used in conjunction with the dummy. The dummy should be weighted with lead to the same weight as the live grenade (4 lb.).

Too much practice cannot be had to ensure length and accuracy of throw.

ADDITIONAL TACTICAL USES OF THE GRENADE

Though the grenade was originally designed for anti-tank work, it could be effectively employed against enemy infantry.

Again, imagination should come into play to devise various uses for the grenade.

The following are a few suggestions:—

Throw from windows on to passing vehicles or infantry.

Throw from bridges or viaducts on to passing vehicles or infantry.

Throw from trees overhanging roads on to vehicles passing underneath. (Don't forget to use a safety strap.) Choose the last vehicle if more than one.

For Demolitions.

The grenade can be used for demolition purposes by removing the "Always Fuse" and using a detonator and a length of time fuse, or by using an electrical demolition set, to explode the detonator. If a considerable charge is required, further grenades can be grouped around the prepared grenade. Bind together with adhesive tape or string. Sympathetic explosion will do the rest.

CHAPTER VI

No. 74 (S.T.) ANTI-TANK GRENADE (GROUP No. 2).

Type – – – –	Hand H.E. 5-seconds delayed action fuse with C.E. pellet booster.
Weight – – –	2¼ lb. Without metal protective casing—2 lbs.
Dimensions – –	9¼ inches in length. 5 inches diameter. Glass flask, 4¼ inches diameter. Throwing handle, 1 inch diameter by 4¼ inches in length.
Explosive Content –	1⅛ lb. nitro-glycerine.

PURPOSE OF DESIGN

To attack and damage armoured fighting vehicles. This grenade possesses a unique feature in the fact that it is designed to stick on to the target. This sticking propensity has its limitations, and the grenade cannot be expected to adhere to a sloping or vertical surface that is contaminated by grease, oil, mud or water; in fact, it would seem best to apply it, if possible, to horizontal surfaces of A.F.V.s such as the engine covering or the top of the turret. It can be thrown short distances by hand, but is best applied by smashing it directly on to the target. It can be thrown or dropped from windows, viaducts, bridges or high banks on to passing vehicles.

It is an exceptionally handy demolition set and can be used to blow in doors in buildings or pill boxes, and to demolish partition walls of buildings, and, therefore, it becomes an excellent weapon for street fighting. It can be used in ambushes and to support road blocks, and is an excellent weapon to use on A.F.V.s, etc., when in harbours during night attacks or fighting patrols.

In an emergency it could be used as an anti-personnel grenade to attack enemy infantry or machine gun posts.

To sum up, the following is a condensed list of some of its many uses:—

Used as an Anti-tank Grenade, it can be applied from—

    (a) Ambushes and road blocks;
    (b) Windows and roofs of buildings;
    (c) Bridges, viaducts, high banks and trees over-hanging roads.

Used as a Demolition Set—

    (a) To apply to stationary vehicles;
    (b) To doors and partition walls;
    (c) To petrol tanks and carriers;
    (d) To damage machinery, etc.

Used as an Anti-personnel Grenade against—

    (a) Lorry-borne infantry;
    (b) Bunched enemy infantry;
    (c) Machine gun and gun positions.

Generally—

For night operations, patrols and finally for guerilla warfare.

RECOGNITION

Live Grenade.—The globular split casing is painted a dark brown colour and is sealed with adhesive tape.

Instructional Grenade.—The casing is painted a similar colour to the live grenade but has stencilled on it in black lettering "INSTRUCTIONAL."

Dummy Grenade.—The dummy grenade for practice-throwing is made of wood and shaped to resemble the live grenade. It is painted white and has a heavy metal ring around the middle of the globe.

Packing.

S.T. grenades are packed in a green, brown-coloured tin box shaped somewhat like an attache case with a carrying handle. Each case contains 5 grenades secured by spring clips and 5 bakelite handles each packed in a cylindrical cardboard carton. On the inside of the lid of the box are found clips to secure a long cardboard cylinder which contains 5 detonator assemblies.

DESCRIPTION OF THE GRENADE

The Body consists of a spherical glass flask which is $4\frac{1}{4}$ inches in diameter and contains $1\frac{1}{8}$ lb. of a specially prepared form of nitro-glycerine, which is, in appearance, a dirty white treacly substance. Formed in the top of the flask is a glass neck about $1\frac{1}{16}$ inches in length and $1\frac{7}{16}$ inches in diameter. It is screw-threaded externally to take the bakelite screwed retaining ring of the handle. Two short projections are formed externally and opposite to one another which serve to help retain the metal casing and also to prevent it rotating, and a shoulder is formed inside the neck to take the flange of the tube which receives the detonator assembly. Around and covering the outside of the flask is a stockinet material impregnated with a solution of birdlime or latex. It is secured around the neck of the flask by a thin brass retaining band.

The flask is sealed at its neck by a rubber disc or plug (sometimes a wooden plug is used), and on top of this is found a fibre board disc or washer. The plug and the washer are retained in position by a screwed bakelite ring. This assembly serves to keep out moisture and also retains the igniter-assembly tube in position. The fibre washer absorbs any small leakage of nitroglycerine.

The Igniter Assembly Tube—$\frac{11}{16}$-inch internal diameter × $2\frac{1}{4}$ inches in length—is constructed from a light aluminium foil and is closed at its bottom end. At the open top end a flange is formed, which fits down on to the shoulder in the neck of the flask. Between the flange and the shoulder is found a thin rubber washer, and the tube fits snugly into the neck of the flask.

The Metal Casing—5 inches in diameter and spherical in shape—is constructed from two light sheet-iron pressings which are held together at their lower ends by a spring-loaded hinge. The two halves are slightly

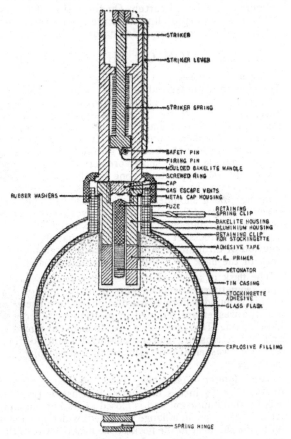

No. 74 (S.T.) ANTI-TANK GRENADE

flanged to form a joint, one within the other, and open vertically. The top ends of each half are shaped and flanged, so that when fitted together they form a narrow collar around the neck of the flask, and in each portion is a recess in the flange which engages with the two projections or nibs on the neck. Two rubber wedged-shaped plugs are found internally on each portion which serves to locate the glass flask and prevent it from adhering to the outer casing.

The outer casing is retained around the neck by a thin brass rip-off tape, at the end of which is a metal finger ring. There are other and alternative securing devices, one of which consists of a short pin and ring and the other a forked-shaped spring clip which engages on the two projections at the neck. Adhesive tape also serves to aid the retaining of the two halves together.

The Throwing Handle is a bakelite moulding 4¼ inches in length and 1 inch in diameter. Internally and throughout its length is formed a sleeve to receive the striker assembly. At its open top end and to one side is moulded an aperture to receive the striker lever. At the bottom end is a flange which receives the screwed bakelite securing ring. Towards the upper end of the striker sleeve is moulded a bush through which the striker runs. This bush is of a slightly larger diameter than the striker, thus allowing room for the gases generated by the exploded cap and burning fuse to escape to the open air. The underside of the bush forms a shoulder against which rests the striker spring. About threequarters down from the top a hole is drilled through the handle to receive the safety pin.

The Striker Assembly consists of a brass striker, striker spring, striker lever and safety pin. The whole assembly operates in the same way as the mechanism of the No. 36 H.E. grenade, already explained in Chapter II. The brass alloy striker is longer than that used in the No. 36, being 3¾ inches overall by $\frac{3}{16}$-inch in diameter; at the top or neck end it is screw-threaded to receive a milled nut, ⅜-inch in diameter, underneath which rests the pronged ends of the striker lever. At the head or lower end a flange is formed, ½-inch long and $\frac{1}{2}$-inch in diameter, which fits snugly into the sleeve; on the face and in the centre of this flange is formed a sharp-pointed cone-shaped firing pin. The upper portion of the flange receives the lower end of the striker spring.

The Striker Spring is the ordinary spiral compression type and is longer and lighter than that used in the No. 36. It is held in compression between the flange of the striker and the underside of the bakelite bush in the handle.

The Striker Lever serves the same purpose as that on the No. 36, but is of a different shape, being $3\frac{3}{8}$ inches in length. At its upper end it is bent sharply over at right angles for threequarters of an inch, and slotted to fit round the neck of the striker; at its lower end it is shaped to fit round the handle and in this portion are a pair of holes to correspond with the pair of holes in the bakelite handle. The safety pin is inserted through these two pairs of holes.

The Safety Pin is a split pin, 2 inches in length, and through the ring at the closed end is attached an oblong tinned tab upon which is painted "To be withdrawn before throwing."

The Detonator Assembly consists of a bakelite housing, percussion cap, 5-seconds fuse, detonator, and a composition exploding pellet and two small rubber bands. The bakelite housing is $\frac{7}{8}$-inch in diameter and $1\frac{3}{8}$ inches in length, and it is moulded with a central sleeve throughout its length. Externally, at the upper end, a flange, $\frac{1}{16}$-inch in diameter by $\frac{1}{4}$-inch in depth, is formed, which rests on the shoulder in the neck of the glass flask and at the upper end of the sleeve is a portion of a larger diameter which forms a housing for the cap assembly. The perimeter of this housing is serrated to form a gas escape for the gases given off by the burning fuse.

The ·410 cap fits in a metal housing, which is a tight fit in the bakelite sleeve; a hole is drilled in its lower end, and a 5-seconds fuse is attached to it at this point. The detonator is crimped to the fuse. The C.E. pellet, $\frac{7}{8}$-inch in diameter and 1 inch in length, fits over

the major part of the detonator and is of the same
diameter as the bakelite housing to which it is attached
by a length of adhesive tape. The two rubber bands are
found around the bakelite housing against the underside
of the flange.

SAFETY PRECAUTIONS

(a) First—see that the grenade is not primed.

(b) Before attaching the bakelite handle, carry out
a striker test, similar to that for the No. 36 grenade.

> *NOTE:*—Use a wooden dowel to push up the
> striker when replacing the striker lever. See that
> the striker is central in the sleeve.

(c) See that the milled nut is screwed firmly on to
the neck of the striker, otherwise it may come adrift,
in which case the striker is held by the safety pin;
therefore, upon its withdrawal the striker will act
prematurely and apart from the striker lever.

(d) Should there be a leakage of nitro-glycerine past
the detonator tube, reject the grenade. Any nitro-
glycerine that may have leaked out may be wiped off
with a rag, whereupon the grenade is again safe to use.
Care should be taken to see that the hands are not
contaminated, as nitro-glycerine is poisonous.

(e) Should the cap project above the face of the bakelite housing, reject the detonator assembly. The reason
for this is—that if the cap is forced down into position
the metal cap housing may be also proud with it, and
so the fuse may be forced down into the detonator,
thus causing a premature explosion. The safest method
to use (though the writer is against any tampering with
this assembly) is first to remove the C.E. pellet and
see if the reason for the cap being proud is due to the
C.E. pellet being too tight a fit around the detonator,
push the cap and housing down into position, reamer
out the hole in the C.E. pellet with a wooden rectifier.
Should it be a tight fit, carefully replace over the
detonator and re-secure with the adhesive tape.

To Assemble and Prime the Grenade.

Unscrew and remove the bakelite screw neck ring,
remove the wooden plug, rubber plug and fibre

absorbent disc and discard. Carefully slide from off the the detonator assembly the cardboard protecting tube and discard. Take up the detonator assembly and space out the two thin rubber bands so that one is about a quarter of an inch away from the shoulder and the other towards the lower end of the bakelite housing. (The reason for doing this is so that the detonator is a snug fit into the sleeve, ensuring that, should the throwing handle come away from the grenade during flight, the detonator assembly will remain secure and, the cap having been struck, the grenade will still function.)

Next, carefully insert the detonator assembly into the aluminium sleeve and press home until the under-side of the flange is in contact with the flange on the sleeve.

Remove the bakelite throwing handle from its card-board container and wrapping, and screw it on to the neck of the grenade and tighten right up. Should the screw ring not attach the handle tightly down on to the neck of the grenade, remove it and select another throwing handle that will fit tightly. The grenade is now primed and assembled.

Mechanism.

Upon the safety pin being withdrawn the grenade is perfectly safe while the hand is gripping the striker lever. Upon the grenade being thrown the striker lever flies off under the influence of the compressed striker spring: the striker is now free to be forced down until the firing pin on its head strikes and fires the cap. The explosion of the cap ignites the fuse, which burns for 5 seconds and explodes the detonator which sets off the C.E. pellet which, in turn, causes the nitro-glycerine filling to explode, thus exploding the grenade.

TO USE THE GRENADE

Prepare to use or throw.—Remove the metal hemi-spheres or protective casing by pulling off the forked spring clip, or by inserting the finger into the ring and pulling off the brass rip tape, or by inserting the finger into the ring and removing the pin, as the case may be. The two halves of the hemisphere under the influence of the spring hinge are now forced open clear of the grenade and fall to the ground.

Throwing the Grenade.

Hold the grenade by gripping the throwing handle with the striker lever well in the palm of the hand and pull out the safety pin, taking great care at the same time to keep the pin secure in the left hand. The grenade can be thrown either underhand or overarm. In both cases a free progressive movement should be used, taking care not to jerk or snatch the grenade, otherwise the throwing handle may break away from the grenade or the glass neck of the flask will be broken, giving the same result.

To place the Grenade on to its Target.

Hold the grenade, as previously mentioned, and smash the grenade on to the target so that the flask is broken and the contents of the stockinet envelope spread over as large a surface as possible. This adds to the cutting effect of the explosion and also gives better adherence on to the target. The striker lever should be released smartly, otherwise half the power of the striker spring is lost.

An alternative method is to grip the handle in the palm of the hand with the top of the throwing handle protruding at the upper portion of the hand (thumb to the top); then stab the grenade downwards on to the target and release lever as before.

The grenade can be thrown without using cover, as the thrower is safe at 20 yards distance from point of impact.

The reason for taking particular care to retain the safety pin is this—that should the grenade be thrown overarm it may attach itself to the back of the shoulder of the thrower, whose predicament would be awkward if the safety pin was not available for re-insertion. When thrown underarm the grenade may become stuck to a leg, when the same thing would apply.

Hint to Instructors.

To impress the point that the safety pin should be retained the following is a useful method to employ:—

Tell the class that the No. 74 is the most wasteful grenade of them all, as you discard the following articles:—the cardboard throwing handle container and corrugated paper wrapping; the cardboard protective cylinder from the igniter assembly; the bakelite screwed retaining ring; rubber and fibre disc washers; the metal protective casing; and, finally, the grenade itself is thrown. The only thing which is NOT thrown away is *THE SAFETY PIN*.

Practice-throwing.

Wooden practice grenades are now issued to the Home Guard, and these should be thrown with a high trajectory, as the grenade should be applied to the top of the tank. Some sort of dummy tank should be set up for this purpose. A good deal of practice is required to become proficient.

Storage.

The grenades should be stored in a dry store, having as even a temperature as possible, and away from the sun, otherwise the expansion of the explosive content and air within the flask force the detonator tube upwards, making the attachment of the throwing handle somewhat awkward and also if the grenades have been stored horizontally some nitro-glycerine may exude. It is best to store the grenades so that the necks of the flasks are upwards. The grenades should be frequently inspected and if leaks take place the faulty ones should be destroyed. On action stations the grenades should be primed ready and placed in a safe place, as the assembly of the grenade is rather a lengthy process.

Method of Carrying.

A proper grenade haversack is, of course, preferable, but a carrier could be improvised from sandbags. Owing to the bulk and weight of the grenade only a few can be carried by any one man.

CHAPTER VII

No. 76 S.I.P. GRENADE (GROUP 2).

Type – – Hand Incendiary and smoke grenade. The contents become ignited on contact with the air. RED or GREEN cap. Self-igniting phosphorus.

Weight – 1¼ lb. ½-pint capacity clear glass bottle.

Dimensions 6¼ inches × 2·7 inches (Red Cap). 6¼ inches × 2·5 inches (Green Cap).

Contents – Half of liquid phosphorus, the remainder being naphtha or benzine with latex (crude rubber) added.

Purpose of Design.

The grenade was originally designed to take the place of the "Molotov Cocktail" to burn out A.F.V.s, and also to put up a smoke screen, and had a red cap. Later, the green cap bottle was introduced, to be fired from the "Northover Projector."

Packing.

The grenades are packed in a wooden case partitioned off (to prevent breakages) to contain 24 grenades. Measurement of box, 21½ inches × 13¾ inches × 9¼ inches. Weight, when filled, 53 lbs. The hinged lid is marked on the outside with — Bombs. Fragile glass. Highly inflammable. Do not drop." Two rope carrying handles are fitted. On the underside of the lid is screwed a metal plate on which are directions as to storage and fire precautions.

Description of Grenade.

The grenade consists of a ½-pint capacity clear glass bottle containing liquid phosphorus, benzine or naphtha and crude rubber (latex) sealed with a RED or GREEN metal crown cork-type cap.

Safety Precautions.

(a) On no account remove the metal caps (otherwise ignition will take place).

(b) On no account should the RED cap grenade be fired from the "Northover Projector." The GREEN cap grenade is the one to be used for this purpose.

Treatment of Burns from Phosphorus.

Any contaminated part should be washed in cold water and kept immersed if possible until thoroughly cleansed. A weak solution of copper sulphate is also effective for this purpose.

APPLICATION OF THE GRENADE

It can be thrown by hand from slit trenches, buildings, bridges, embankments, viaducts, on to A.F.V.s or into buildings to burn out the defenders.

It can be used effectively as a smoke screen to blind enemy observation or return fire.

It is also useful to use in conjunction with "Molotov Cocktails" to cause their ignition.

The above purpose can also be fulfilled by firing the Green Cap grenade from the "Northover Projector."

Paper cylinders with a fibre board ring at the bottom are now issued, into which the Green Cap No. 76 Grenade is inserted and secured by adhesive paper before firing from the "Northover Projector." By this method many breakages are prevented.

The grenade should be thrown sharply against the target to ensure breakage of the bottle, thus allowing the contents to ignite.

Do not shake the bottles before throwing or firing, otherwise the liquid phosphorus will be coated by the latex-benzine solution and thus cause delay in the ignition of their contents.

Storage.

The grenades should be stored in a non-inflammable store, and frequent inspection should be made to ensure that the caps do not become rusty otherwise a fire will result upon the caps becoming perforated. Should the store be damp or open to the weather, the caps should be coated with a special composition provided for this purpose. Should this not be available, they can be dipped into slightly warmed dubbin or tallow. Any thick tacky grease will also serve the purpose.

Method of Carrying.

The box provided seems to be the best means of transportation. This means a two-man load.

CHAPTER VIII.

THE MOLOTOV COCKTAIL.

Group No. 2 and 3 – Anti-tank and incendiary bomb.

Weight (approx.) –   1 pint bottle. Quart bottle.

Inflammatory Content   Petrol and/or tar, creosote, sump oil or Diesel oil.

Fuse – – – – – Pre-ignited to cause combustion of contents upon bottle being broken on target.

GENERAL DESCRIPTION

The "Molotov Cocktail," sometimes referred to as the Petrol Bottle Bomb, is a simple type of fire bomb, which is easily manufactured from readily obtainable materials found in any inhabited neighbourhood. At the outset of this war it constituted the main offensive weapon, in the hands of the Home Guard, against A.F.V.s. This type of fire bomb was used with success in both the Spanish and Finnish wars. Although, since the aforementioned wars, tank design has improved considerably, the "Molotov Cocktail" should still be a part of Home Guard equipment to augment other anti-tank weapons that are now issued. The use of this weapon immediately places the crew of the enemy vehicle on the defensive, causing them to close their hatches, and fogging their visibility by smoke and flame. Used in sufficient quantities, it might be the means of destroying the most modern of tanks.

The attacking force should aim at enveloping the A.F.V. in smoke and flame, and the ground around, and particularly in the path of the tank, should be covered by burning petrol and oil. For this purpose, drums and buckets of petrol and tar mixture should be at hand to use in conjunction with the "Molotov Cocktail."

METHOD OF CONSTRUCTION AND ALTERNATIVE MATERIALS

The first essential is a pint-capacity bottle of the ordinary beer-bottle variety. The bottle should be deeply scored with a glass cutter to ensure its breakage upon hitting the target. The best way to do this is to score two lateral lines around the circumference of the bottle about $2\frac{1}{2}$ inches apart, and then fill in between them with a series of crosses reaching from the top to the bottom line. An extra set of scorings can be added if a quart bottle is used. A screw-stopper bottle is the best, but corks can be used where the former are not available.

The bottle should be just over threequarters filled with 25 per cent. petrol and 75 per cent. water-gas tar. Alternative fillings to use in conjunction with petrol are old sump oil, creosote or Diesel oil. The less inflammable the contents the more petrol is required. Bottles should be selected that are easily broken, such as beer, whisky, gin, wine or lime-juice bottles. Large bottles such as quart champagne and beer bottles are harder to throw and are not so easily broken. When stoppered the bottle should be air and leak proof. The above fillings are only a suggestion, and further fillings can be used if desired and if more readily available.

Fuses.

One or two types of fuse have been issued to the Home Guard, and if sufficient of these are available no alternative is required.

As an alternative to the manufactured fuse the following are a few easily prepared: a wad of cotton-waste, attached to the bottle by adhesive tape, forms a handy fuse. Before throwing, the cotton-waste is soaked with petrol or paraffin and lit. The big fault with this fuse is that it may give a position away at night.

A length of cinematograph film wound round and attached to the bottle makes a handy fuse, but with the same drawbacks as the cotton-waste.

The best method seems to be to use a self-igniting fuse.

A self-igniting "Molotov" can be constructed as follows:—

Use the same bottle, preparation and filling as before. Make up a mixture of chlorate of potash and sugar ground together. Spread the mixture over a stout piece of paper treated with an adhesive substance so that the mixture sticks on. Wrap the prepared paper, mixture inwards, around the bottle and attach by string or adhesive tape; in addition, attach a small bottle, phial or test tube containing about an egg-cupfull of commercial sulphuric acid to the bottle. Upon the acid bottle breaking the acid in contact with the chlorate of potash causes combustion.

Another method is to include an eggcupfull of sulphuric acid with the mixture in the bottle with the same result. The only drawback with this method is that the acid deteriorates after about .30 days or so. Therefore, Cocktails so treated should not be stored longer than this period.

TACTICAL USES

The "Molotov Cocktail" should be used in ambushes when the A.F.V. is slowed down or stopped. A good supply of petrol and tar mixture in drums should be available to use in conjunction with the bomb to surround the tank with flame and smoke. Wherever possible, the position should be arranged so that the Cocktails are thrown down on to the tank. Cover can be provided by a simple circular hole in the ground about 3 ft. deep and just large enough for a man to crouch down in. In daylight practice should be obtained so that a quick look in the direction of the tank is all that is necessary, deliver the bomb and duck under cover.

Another useful trench to bomb from is the (+) trench, consisting of two trenches 7 to 8 ft. in length crossing one another, and 2 ft. 6 ins. wide and about 3 ft. deep. From this type of trench all points of the compass are covered.

The Cocktail can be thrown from windows or from behind walls in street fighting. Viaducts, bridges and high banks also come in useful for this purpose. The following table is a rough guide to the number of bombs required for certain vehicles:—

Armoured cars and light tanks ...	At least 8
Heavy and medium tanks	,, 12
Cars...	,, 2

Use the Cocktail as a surprise weapon. After the first bomb has reached the target and is alight, it is unnecessary to ignite the fuses of the grenades that follow. A handy method of attack is to first throw a 76 S.I.P. grenade and then follow with "Molotovs."

Practice-Throwing.

Plenty of practice should be had with sand-filled bottles, using a canvas screen as a target. If the practice site is chosen on soft or sandy soil but few bottles should be broken. A moving target should also be used. "Molotovs" are not easy to throw, and constant practice is required to gain proficiency.

Storage.

Store the bombs in as dry and cool a place as possible, as damp will affect the fuses and wet bottles are difficult to handle when throwing.

Method of Carrying.

A box made up, beer crate fashion, to hold six bombs, with a stout rope handle, seems to be the best method of transportation.

CHAPTER IX

GERMAN HAND GRENÀDES.

Should the Home Guard come into action, a knowledge of enemy hand grenades, in addition to our own,
would prove invaluable. The German soldier, particularly the parachutist and air-borne troops, seem to
be well equipped with hand grenades, and these
falling into the hands of the Home Guard might well
serve to overcome any shortage of, or to conserve,
our own supplies.

The German hand grenades described in the following
pages are the three that would be most likely to be
encountered, and even a small knowledge of them might
be the means of saving Home Guards frbm enemy
booby traps.

THE No. 24 STICK HAND GRENADE.

Group No. 1	–	Anti-personnel.
Weight – – –		1 lb. 5 oz.
Dimensions – –		1 ft. 2 inches overall length. Body approx. 2¼ inches diameter × 4 inches in length. Handle 10 inches in length.
Explosive content		6 oz. of T.N.T.
Lethal effect – –		By blast. 50 ft. radius.
Type – – – –		Delayed action by time fuse. 5½ secs. delay.

Purpose of Design.

This grenade is designed for offence: having a thin
steel casing, it relies mainly on blast for its lethal effect,
and can be used by troops advancing in the open owing

to the fact that it can be thrown to a greater distance than its effective lethal area. It can also be used singly or in groups for demolition purposes. In the latter case the handles are removed from the grenades with the exception of one. They are then bound together with the grenade with handle attached in the centre of the group. In this manner they can be used against tanks, pillboxes, etc.

Recognition.

The cylindrical sheet metal body is coloured dark grey-green and attached to this is a 10-inch wooden handle. The grenade is marked "STIEL HAND GRANATE No. 24." (*See frontispiece, page ii.*)

Description.

The body or head of the grenade is constructed from thin iron or steel, and contains the explosive filling. Running down into the explosive is a detonator tube or holder. The 10-inch wooden throwing handle is shaped to form a grip and is hollowed throughout its length to form a sleeve. At the bottom end, which is screw-threaded to screw on to the body, is found exposed the metal end of the delay fuse which receives the detonator. Running through the bore is a double length of cord attached at one end to a lead ball, which is, in turn, attached to the friction igniter and at the other to a porcelain bead, which is retained by a spring-supported disc.

A screw cap fits over the end of the handle to seal it from moisture and to retain the porcelain head.

To prime the grenade.

(a) Unscrew the wooden throwing handle from the head, thus exposing the metal end of the delay action fuse.

(b) Place the detonator into the end of the fuse.

(c) Re-screw the handle on to the body.

The grenade is now primed ready for action.

To throw the grenade.

(a) Unscrew the metal screw cap, thus exposing the porcelain bead.

(b) Pull on the porcelain bead.

Method of Operation.

The bead, being attached to the double cord, when pulled, operates the friction igniter which ignites the fuse, which burns for $5\frac{1}{2}$ seconds and then sets off the detonator which, in turn, sets off the main H.E. filling, thus exploding the grenade.

SMOKE HAND GRENADE

This consists of the Standard Stick grenade. In lieu of H.E. the body is filled with a smoke mixture. A broken white band around the body, near its base, and the letters N.B. in white indicate a smoke grenade.

P.H. 39 STICK HAND GRENADE.

Group No. 1	–	Anti-personnel.
Weight – – –		1 lb. 6 oz.
Dimensions – –		1 ft. 4 inches in length overall. Handle 10 inches in length. Body approx. $2\frac{3}{4}$ inches in diameter × 6 inches in length.
Explosive content		7 oz. T.N.T.
Lethal effect – –		By blast. 50 ft. radius.
Type – – – –		Delayed action by time fuse. $4\frac{1}{2}$ seconds delay.

NOTE:—Apart from the above details the grenade is exactly similar to the No. 24 except that the double cord is attached directly to the metal screw-cap and no porcelain bead is used.

To throw the grenade.—Unscrew the cap from the handle and pull.

GERMAN EGG BOMB.

Group No. 1	–	Anti-personnel.
Weight – – –		12 oz.

Dimensions – –	Approx. 3¼ inches in length overall × 2¼ inches around band.
Explosive content	Gelignite.
Lethal effect – –	By blast.
Type – – – –	Delayed action by time fuse. 5 seconds delay.

Purpose of Design.

This grenade is designed for offence and defence, and relies mainly on blast for its lethal effect. Owing to its light weight (12 oz.), it has a comparatively long range and a fair number can be carried.

Recognition.

The grenade is ovoid in shape with a raised band around its middle, and is painted a dark grey-green. The sealing cap on top is painted a light greeny-blue and is marked 538 A 157. On the band around the middle is marked D0 1940, and on the base is marked 538 A 189.

Description.

The body of the grenade is ovoid in shape with a raised band around its middle. Running down inside

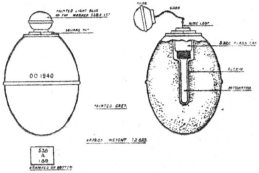

GERMAN EGG HAND GRENADE

into the explosive content is a detonator tube or sleeve. Screwed into this sleeve by either a square or a wing nut is the time mechanism, which consists of a

5-seconds delay action flash cap, to which is attached a length of wire. The wire, in turn, is attached to the push on sealing cap.

To Prime the Grenade.

(a) Unscrew the mechanism holder.

(b) Unscrew the protective cap, which is found on the end of the flash cap thus exposed.

(c) Take a detonator from its box and carefully slip it on to the flash cap.

(d) Screw the whole fuse assembly back with the wing nut or square nut, using the spanner provided for this purpose.

The grenade is now primed ready for action.

Safety Precautions.

See that the detonator tube or pocket is free from dirt and obstructions.

See that the open end of the detonator is free from dust or obstructions. It it is not, reject it.

To Throw the Grenade.

Before throwing the grenade, slip off the cap and pull; then throw.

Method of Operation.

Pulling on the cap to which a wire is attached operates the flash cap, which has a delay action of 5 seconds. The detonator is then set off which sets off the main filling, thus explosing the grenade.

> *NOTE:*—There is another grenade (of the egg variety) carried by parachutists which is operated by tapping, after removal of the cap. This grenade has a delayed action of 3 seconds only and is filled with a lachrymatory gas. Care is required tackling an enemy armed with this grenade, as he may have his hands up as if surrendering, and concealed in his hands may be one or two of these grenades, which be ignites by striking on his own steel helmet.

CHAPTER X

No. 69 H.E. GRENADE (BAKELITE)

Type: Hand, blast, percussion, H.E. (explodes on impact).
Weight: 1 lb. (approx.).   *Dimensions:* 4⅛ × 2⅜ ins. approx
Explosive content: 4 oz. Baratol, or other H.E. fillings.
Lethal effect: By blast.
Packing: 34 in a box, with two boxes containing 17 detonators
in each.

Purpose of design. This grenade was designed for offensive
action against enemy troops. It can be thrown in the open,
without injury to the thrower, owing to its limited blast area.
It is used more to create a demoralising effect rather than for
its lethal capacity, which is small. Being light and having a
smooth exterior, a fair number can be carried; therefore, it is
particularly useful for patrols. It can be used for training
purposes, but, in this case, should be thrown *behind* troops, as
the lead alloy ball may fly out and cause injuries.

Recognition. The live grenade is black and has a series of red
crosses around the top of the body of the grenade, and around
the middle is a coloured band denoting the type of explosive
content.

Description (see drawing, page 75). The cylindrical ovoid body
is moulded bakelite and through its centre runs a varnished
paper detonator sleeve. This sleeve is sealed at its bottom end by
a bakelite base plug which is fitted with a rubber plug for retaining
the detonator in position. At the top of the body is screwed the
"Always Fuse"; a rubber sealing washer is fitted between the
fuse-holder and the body to exclude moisture and to act as a
spring washer. The "Always Fuse" is fully described on pages 43,
44 and 45, and is identical to that fitted to the No. 73 Anti-tank
Grenade.

Priming the Grenade. To prime the grenade, unscrew the base
plug and examine the detonator sleeve for obstruction; remove
any resinous grease and insert the detonator *open end first.*
Replace the base plug and screw fully home.

Safety Precautions. First, remove base plug and make sure
that grenade is not primed. Before throwing be sure that tape and
safety bolt are in position. Stripping is forbidden.

Method of Throwing. Remove the adhesive tape from safety
cap, retain tape and bob-weight in position by forefinger and
thumb and throw by any convenient method (see Training on
35 H.E. Grenade). A left-handed man can hold grenade upside
down and retain the tape and bob-weight with the little finger.
Spin the grenade when throwing for short distances.

Drill. *"Ready"*—Pick up grenade, remove the adhesive tape.
Face the target and turn to right.

   "Throw"—Remove the safety cap, holding the safety
   tape in position and throw.

CHAPTER XI

No. 68 ANTI-TANK GRENADE (GROUP 2)

Type: Blast percussion. (Fired from the Cup Discharger).
Weight: 1¾ lb.   *Dimensions:* 6½ ins. × 2½ ins.
Explosive content: 5 oz. Lyddite or other H.E. fillings.
Packing: 17 in a metal box. Range (effective): 50 to 75 yards.

Purpose of design. To engage A.F.V.s. It is also useful against pill boxes and to engage enemy ensconced in buildings. It is fired from the Cup Discharger (see pages 37, 38 and 39).

Recognition. The live grenade is buff in colour and has a red band round the top and a series of coloured bands around the middle, denoting the explosive contents. The Drill, or dummy, grenade is painted white.

Description (see drawing, page 75). It consists of a cylindrical metal body which is open at its top end and is threaded externally to receive the screw-on cap. Inside is found a cup or liner which with the brass sealing disc and fibre washer is held in position by the screw-on cap. The body is shaped in at the bottom and is threaded internally to receive the tail unit. Tightly packed in the body and surround the liner is the H.E. filling. At the top of the tail tube and projecting into the H.E. filling is the C.E. Pellet container. The tail unit consists of a central mechanism sleeve and 4 vanes (to steady the grenade in flight); at the bottom is fitted a gas check. Screwed into the top of the sleeve is the cap pellet; bearing against this is a tapered creep-spring which is attached at its lower end to the heavy striker. The striker has, at its head, a sharp pointed projection, which fires the cap. Through the centre is a hole to receive the safety pin; below this and running diagonally opposite is a hole to receive the shear wire. Two pairs of holes in the tail tube register with the holes in the striker. The safety pin and the shear wire retain the striker in position. The grenade is already primed.

Safety Precautions. No stripping allowed. Remove the safety pin *just* before inserting into the cup. Make sure that the shear wire is in position. The ends (turned over) of this can be seen each side of the tail tube.

To Fire. Remove the safety pin and insert the grenade into the discharger *TAIL UNIT FIRST* and push fully home. The body of the grenade is now exposed outside the discharger.

Action. The shock of discharge causes the heavy striker to shear the shear wire. The striker, during flight, rests against the bottom of the striker sleeve and is held in position by the creep-spring. On striking the target the heavy striker overcomes the tension of the creep-spring and strikes and fires the cap which explodes the C.E. Pellet exploder, in turn setting off the main H.E. filling. The force of the explosion will penetrate 1½-in. armour plating.

NOTE:—Though the grenade can be fired by one man, by far the best method is to use a loader and a firer.

For application: See EY Rifle and Cup Discharger (Chapter IV).

CHAPTER XII

No. 75 GRENADE (HAWKINS)

Type: Group 2. Anti-tank mine grenade. Exploded by crushing. Hand grenade or mine. Blast.

Weight: 2¼ lb. *Dimensions:* 7½ ins. × 3½ ins. × 2¼ ins. (approx.).

Explosive content: 1¼ lb. Ammonal 704 (B). Insensitive to rifle bullets. 4 oz. "Victor Powder."

Packing: 12 in metal box. G.70 with 24 detonator assemblies.

Purpose of design. This is a small mine with several uses:—

(a) It can be thrown up to 25 yards under the track of a vehicle (from ambush).

(b) Can be attached to Dannert wire.

(c) Can be laid in minefields as ordinary mines, or stacked together to form a composite mine of any power required.

(d) Can be used as a demolition charge.

(e) Can be laid in fords. It is waterproof for a fair period.

Recognition. The live mine grenade is coloured khaki-green and has a red band round it. The dummy grenade is painted a reddish brown and has a white filler cap and a white band across the top and bottom.

Description. The body consists of a one-pint capacity talcum powder type tin (rounded sides) with a screwed filler neck and cap at one end. The body contains the H.E. and the Victor Powder which ensures detonation. Attached to brackets on one of the two broader sides is a plate running almost the length of the body. Across this plate, from side to side, is formed a V-shaped striker. Attached to the body under the striker are two pockets which are sealed at one end, and at the other end have two metal tabs which are bent over to retain the igniter sets in position. Each pocket has an aperture cut out of it which registers under the striker.

The Bickford Igniter Set consists of a tin plate tube flattened at one end. About halfway down inside the tube is fixed a composite and highly inflammable flash pellet. Against this pellet, towards the flattened end of the tube, is a small glass capsule containing sulphuric acid. This capsule is held in position and normally protected from breakage by a fibrous substance like cotton wool. The open end of the tube is large enough to receive a No. 27 or No. 8 mark VII detonator. Around the tube is wound a rolled-up rubber tube.

To assemble the Igniter Set. Insert the detonator into the open end of the tube and unroll the rubber tube to retain the detonator in position and to render the whole assembly waterproof. The flattened tube is painted red.

To prime the Mine. Take the two assembled Igniter Sets and place them through the two holes in the bracket into the two Igniter pockets with the detonators to the front. Then bend over the two metal tabs to retain the Igniters in position. When correctly placed the red portion of the Igniter Sets should show through the two apertures in the pockets.

Action. Whichever way the grenade is thrown, owing to its shape, it will land the right way up. Upon the A.F.V. running over it the weight will force the V-shaped striker down on to the two Igniter Sets through the apertures in the pockets, thus crushing the Bickford Igniters, causing the glass capsules to break and releasing the sulphuric acid. This impinges on to the composite pellets causing them instantly to ignite and in turn exploding the detonators which set off the "Victor Powder." This in turn explodes the H.E. filling.

Safety Precautions. See whether the grenade is primed or not. Handle the Igniter Sets with care. When laying a minefield immediately take the map reference and notify all concerned.

The 75A Grenade is a slight variation on the 75 and has the letter "A" stencilled on it.

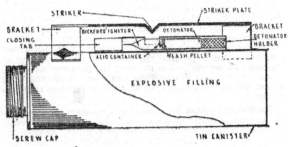

No. 75 Grenade (Mine)—"Hawkins"

See Chapter XII.

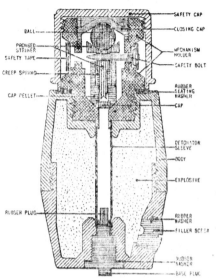

SAFETY CAP
CLOSING CAP
BALL
PRONGED STRIKER
SAFETY TAPE
MECHANISM HOLDER
SAFETY BOLT
CREEP SPRING
RUBBER SEATING WASHER
CAP PELLET
CAP
DETONATOR SLEEVE
BODY
EXPLOSIVE
RUBBER PLUG
RUBBER WASHER
FILLER SCREW
RUBBER WASHER
BASE PLUG

No. 69
BAKELITE
GRENADE.

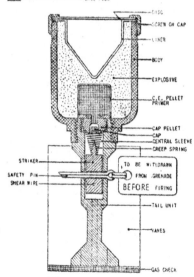

DISC
SCREW ON CAP
LINER
BODY
EXPLOSIVE
C.E. PELLET PRIMER
CAP PELLET
CAP
CENTRAL SLEEVE
CREEP SPRING
STRIKER
SAFETY PIN
SHEAR WIRE
TO BE WITHDRAWN FROM GRENADE BEFORE FIRING
TAIL UNIT
VANES
GAS CHECK

No. 68 ANTI-TANK
GRENADE (RIFLE)

75